D0450603

FIRST GRAPHICS

MY COMMUNITY

WORKING ON THE FARM

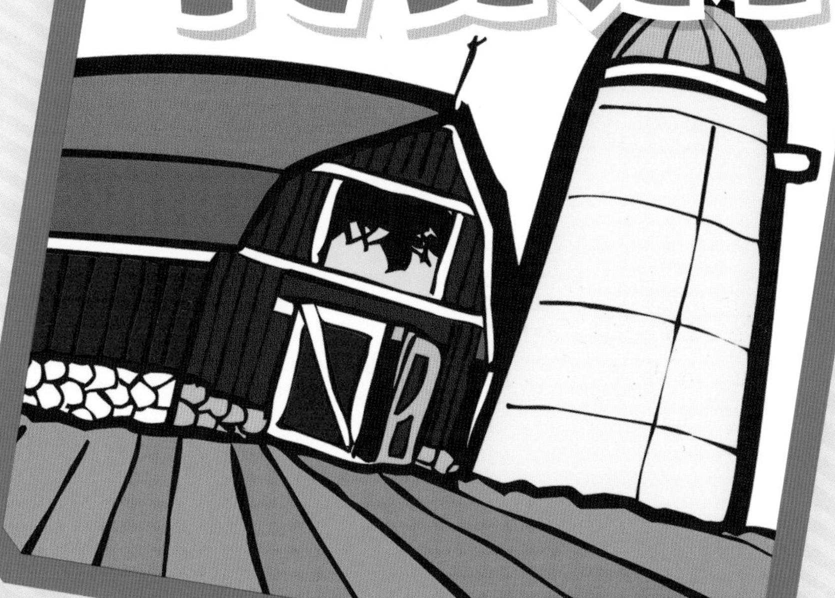

BY LORI MORTENSEN

ILLUSTRATED BY
JEFFREY THOMPSON

Consultant: Karin Schaefer
Minnesota Farm Bureau Federation
Special Programs Coordinator

CAPSTONE PRESS
a capstone imprint

First Graphics are published by Capstone Press,
151 Good Counsel Drive, P.O. Box 669, Mankato, Minnesota 56002.
www.capstonepub.com

Printed in the United States of America in Stevens Point, Wisconsin.

032010
005741WZF10

Books published by Capstone Press are manufactured with paper
containing at least 10 percent post-consumer waste.

Library of Congress Cataloging-in-Publication Data

Mortensen, Lori.
Working on the farm / by Lori Mortensen ; illustrated by Jeffrey Thompson.
p. cm.—(First graphics. My community)
Includes bibliographical references and index.
ISBN 978-1-4296-4510-2 (library binding)
ISBN 978-1-4296-5616-0 (paperback)
1. Farms—Comic books, strips, etc—Juvenile literature. 2. Agriculture—Comic
books, strips, etc—Juvenile literature. I. Title. II. Series.
S519.M68 2011 2009051475
630—dc22

Editor: **Erika L. Shores**
Designer: **Alison Thiele**
Art Director: **Nathan Gassman**
Production Specialist: **Laura Manthe**

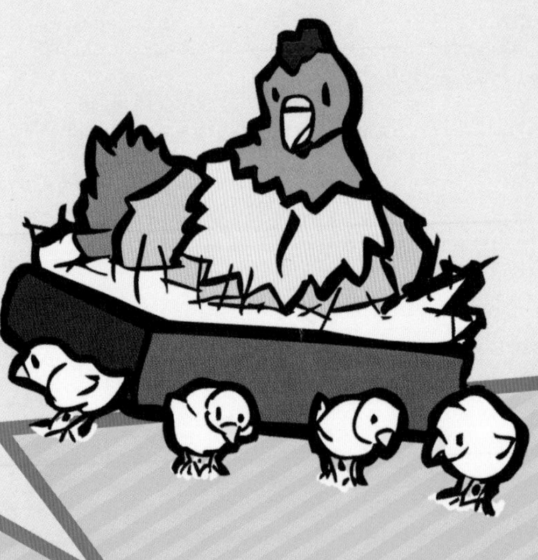

TABLE OF CONTENTS

ON THE FARM

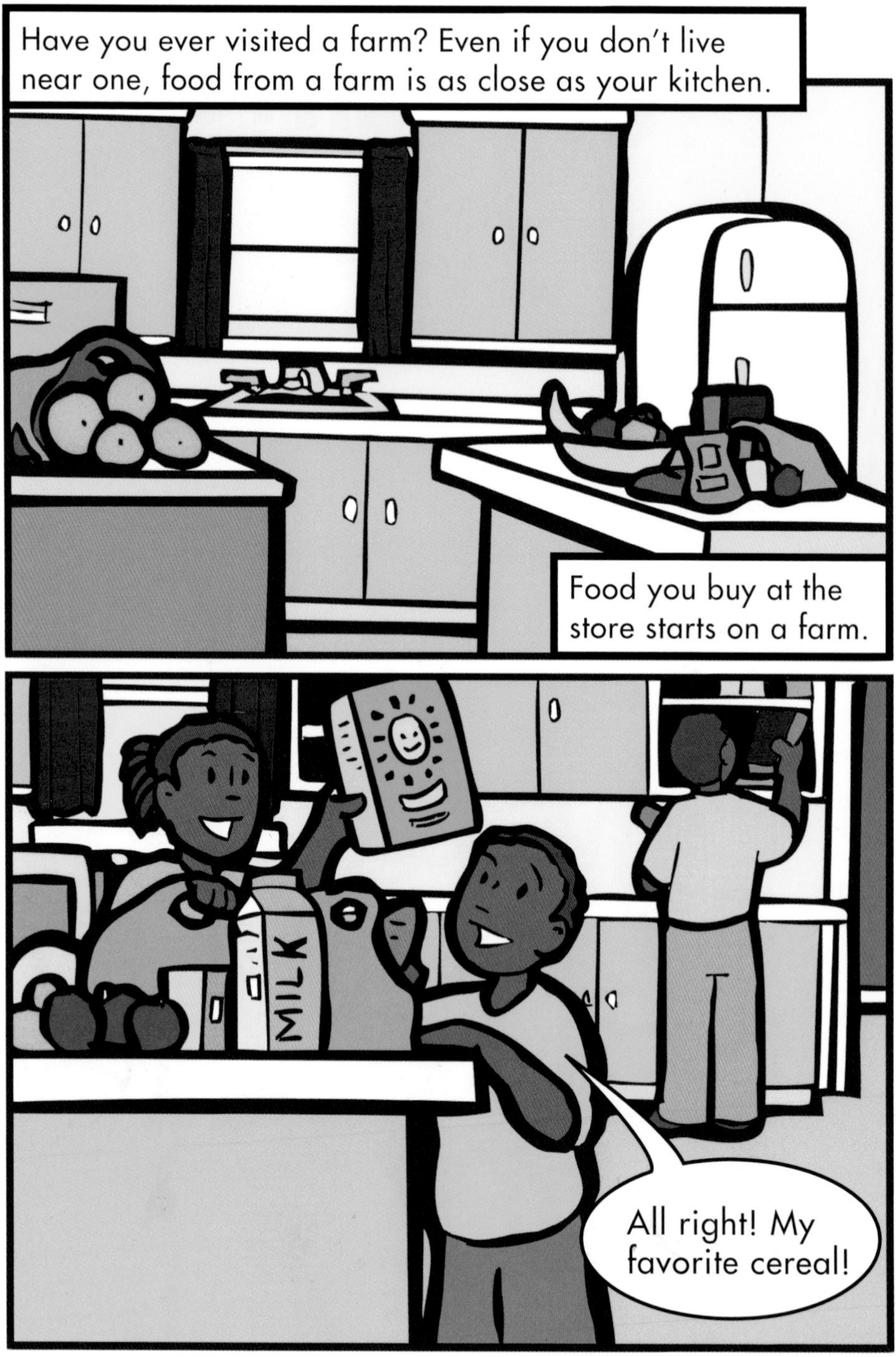

Have you ever visited a farm? Even if you don't live near one, food from a farm is as close as your kitchen.
Food you buy at the store starts on a farm.
MILK
All right! My favorite cereal!

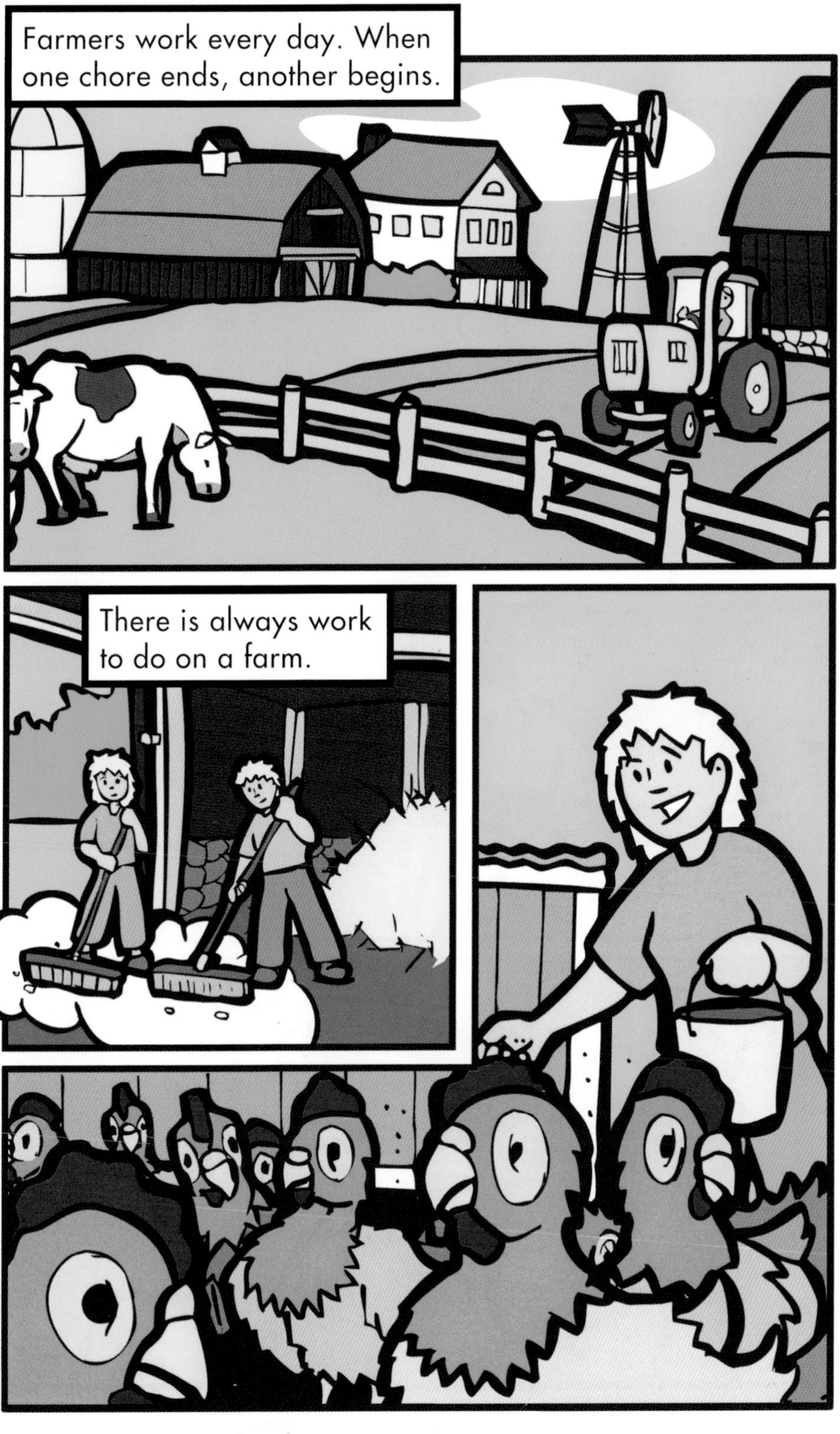
Farmers work every day. When one chore ends, another begins.
There is always work to do on a farm.

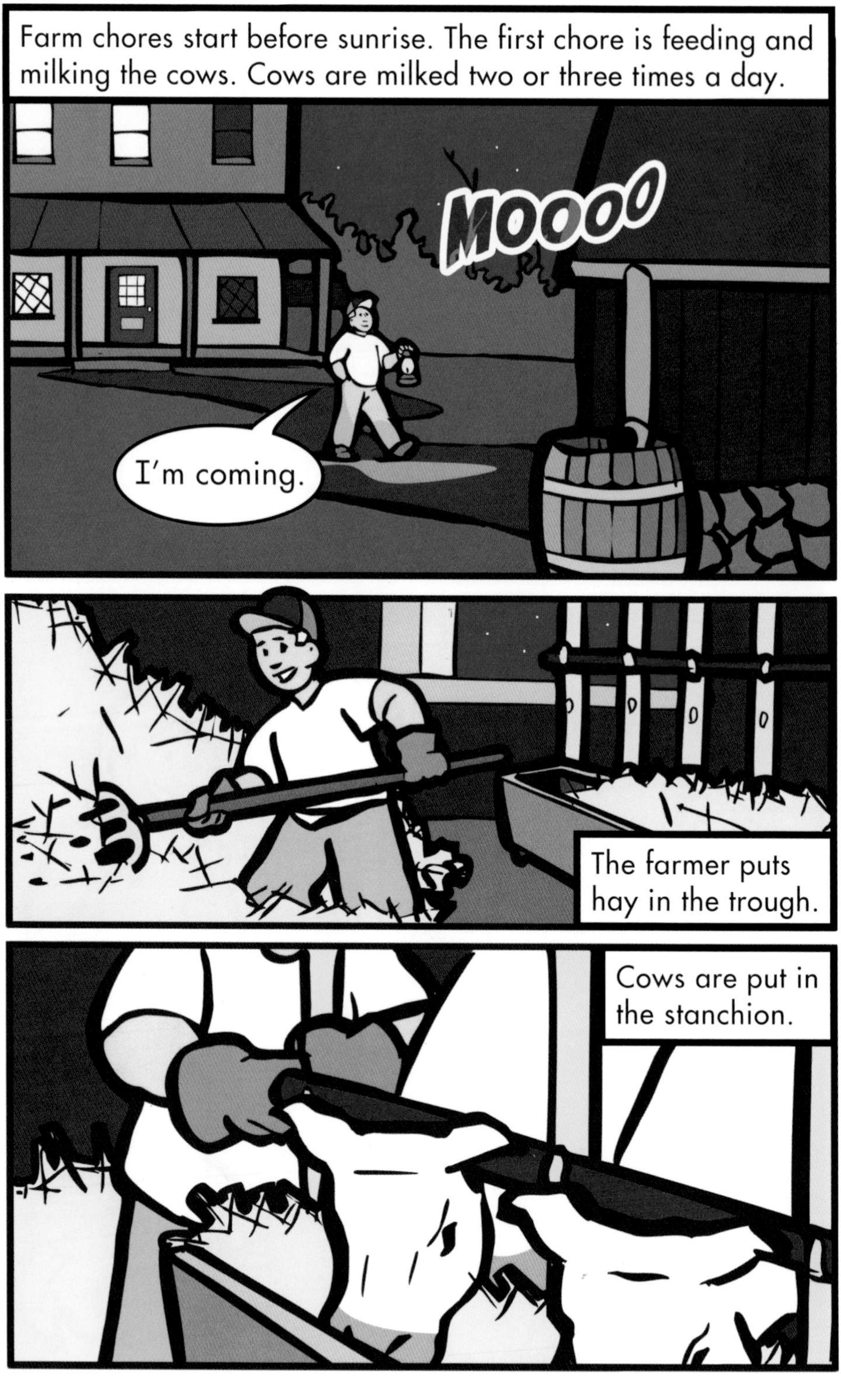
Farm chores start before sunrise. The first chore is feeding and milking the cows. Cows are milked two or three times a day.
MOOOO
I'm coming.
The farmer puts hay in the trough.
Cows are put in the stanchion.

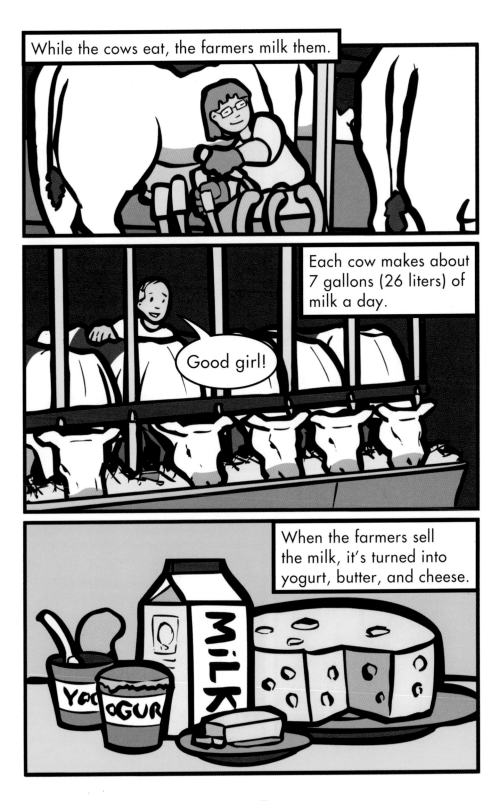

While the cows eat, the farmers milk them.

Each cow makes about 7 gallons (26 liters) of milk a day.

Good girl!

When the farmers sell the milk, it's turned into yogurt, butter, and cheese.

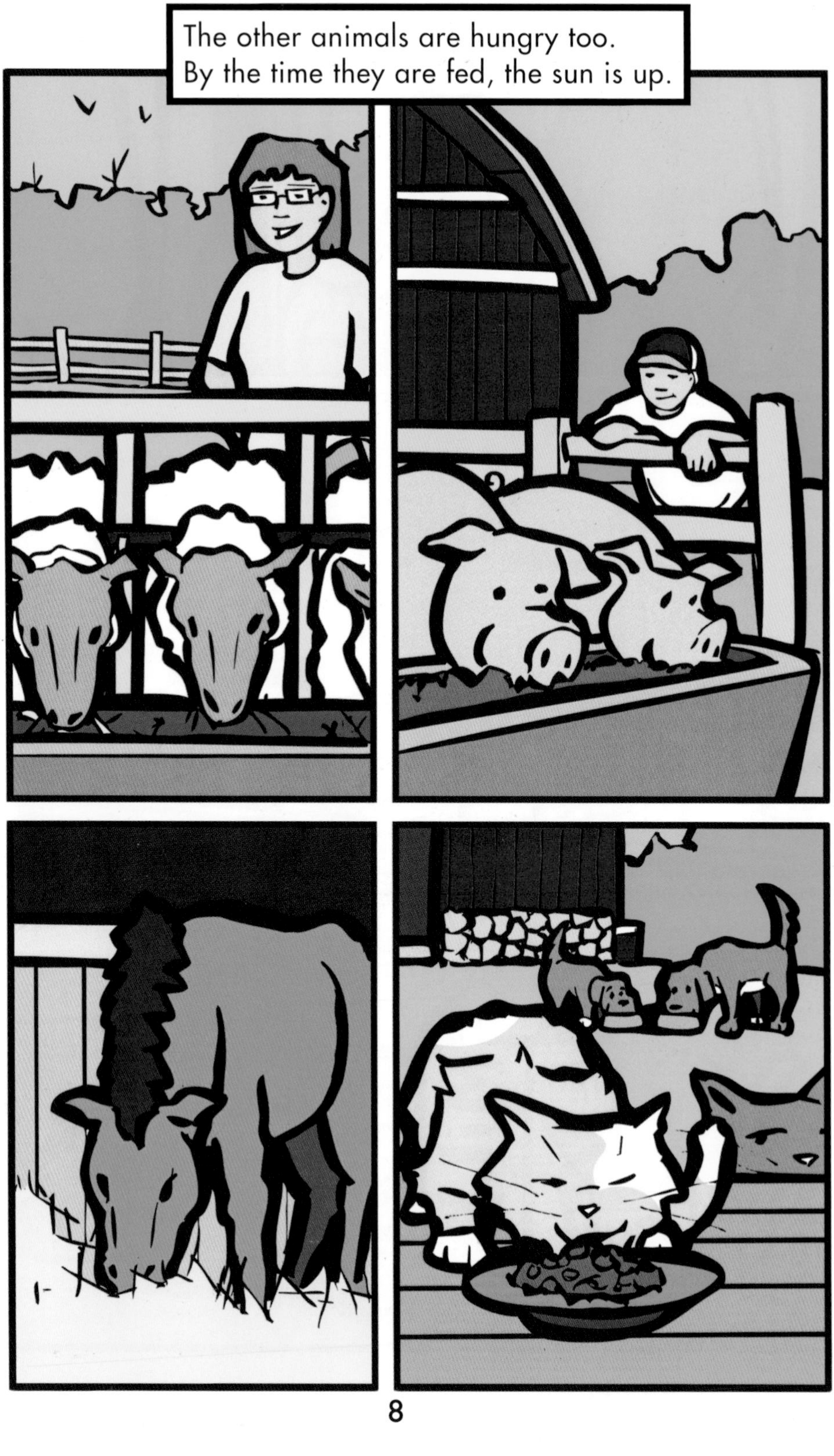
The other animals are hungry too.
By the time they are fed, the sun is up.

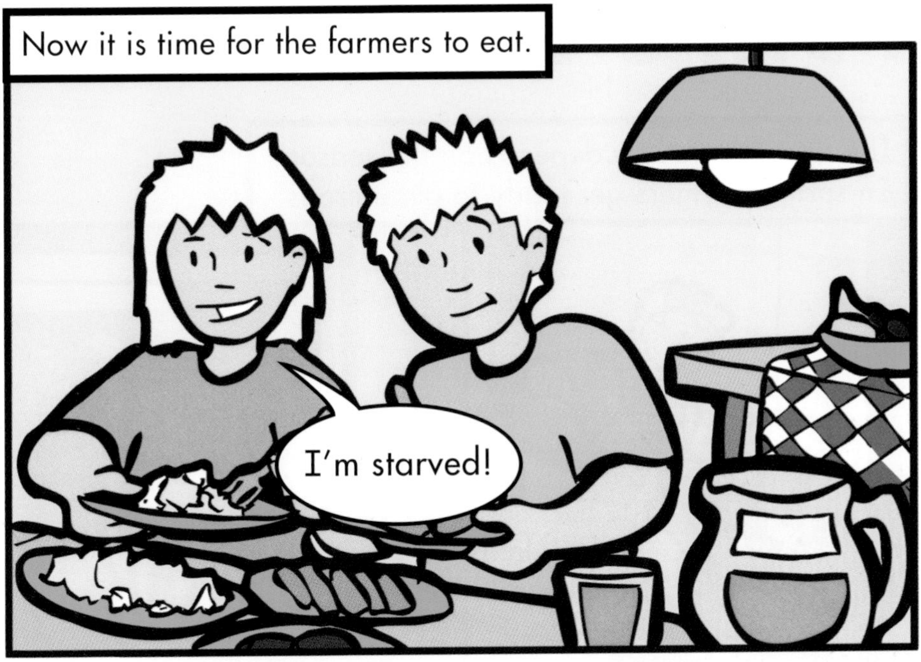
Now it is time for the farmers to eat.
I'm starved!

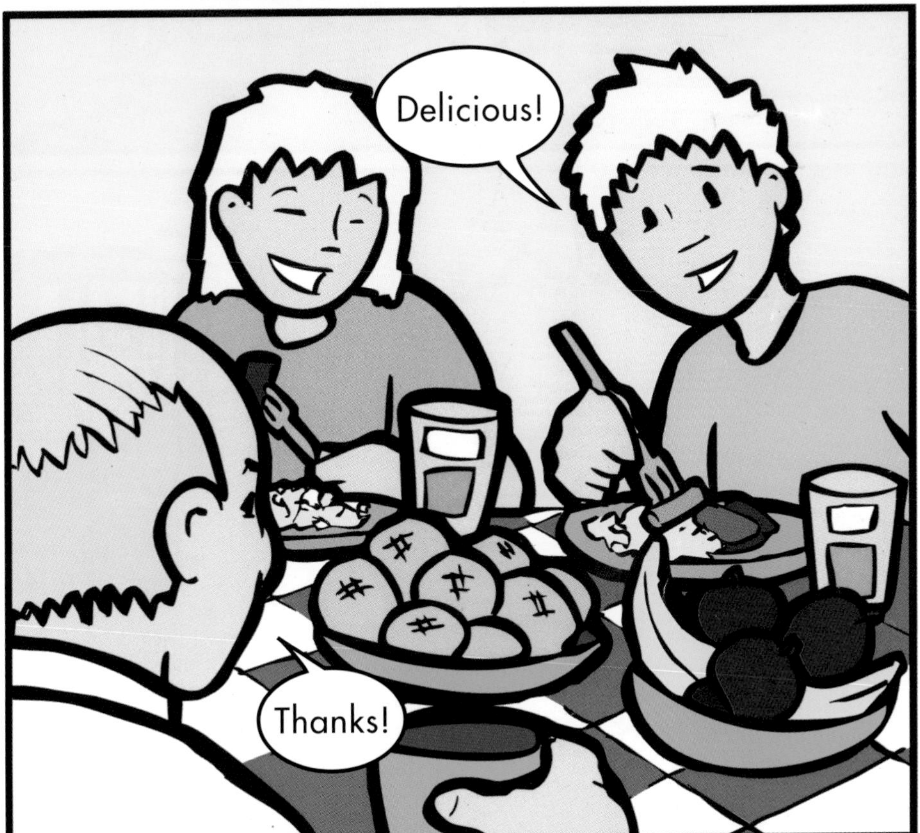
Delicious!
Thanks!

A Day's Work

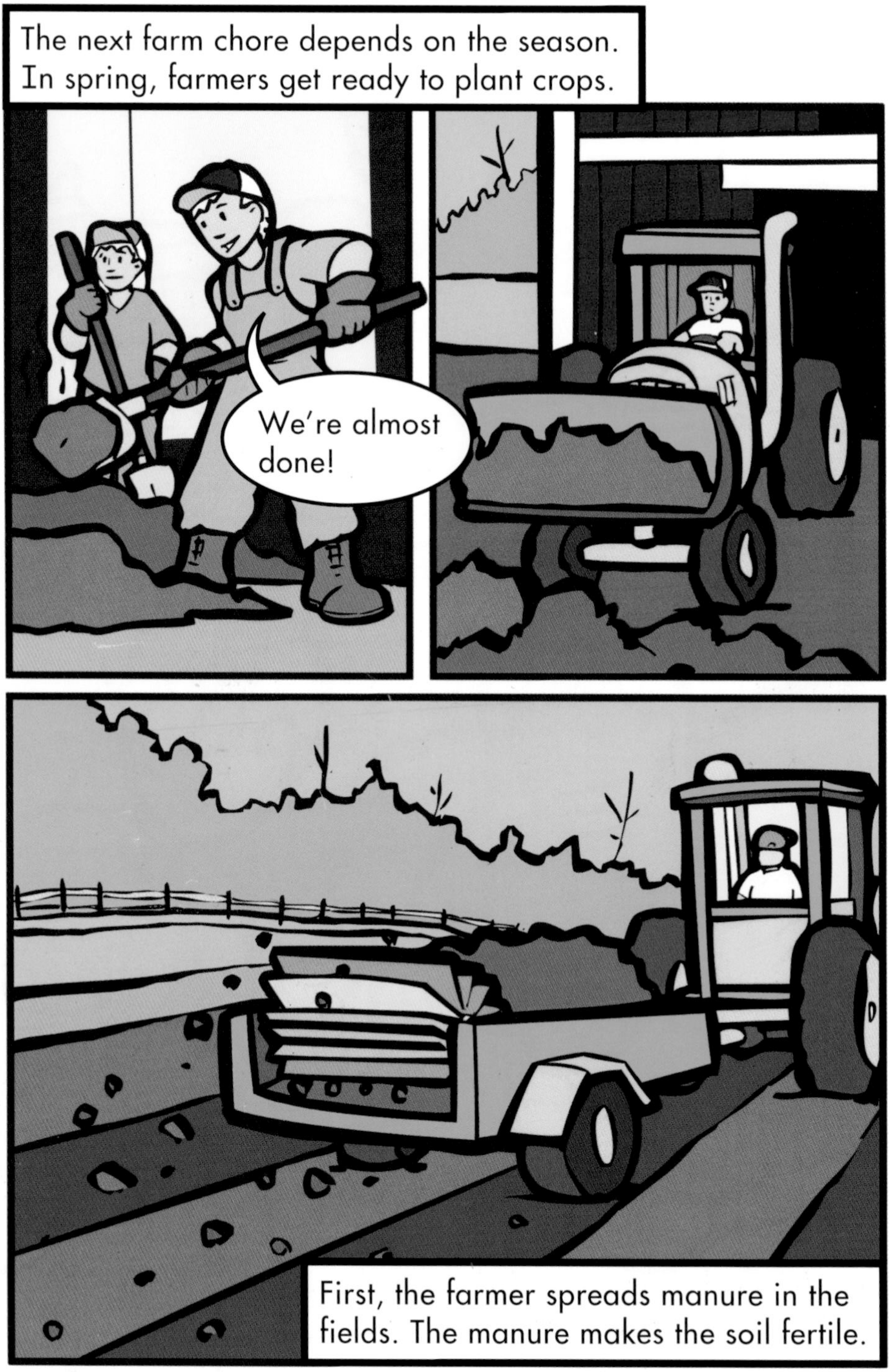
The next farm chore depends on the season. In spring, farmers get ready to plant crops.
We're almost done!
First, the farmer spreads manure in the fields. The manure makes the soil fertile.

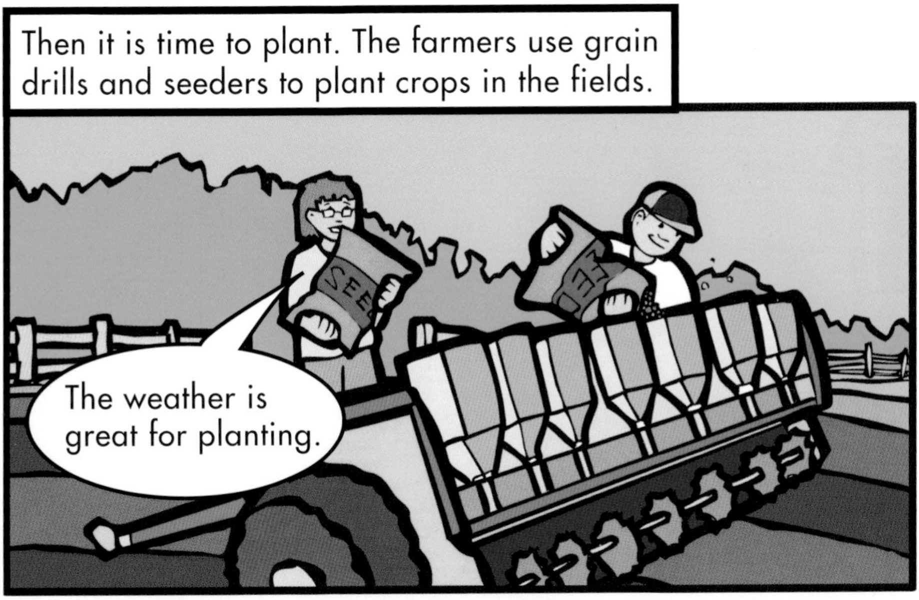
Then it is time to plant. The farmers use grain drills and seeders to plant crops in the fields.
The weather is great for planting.

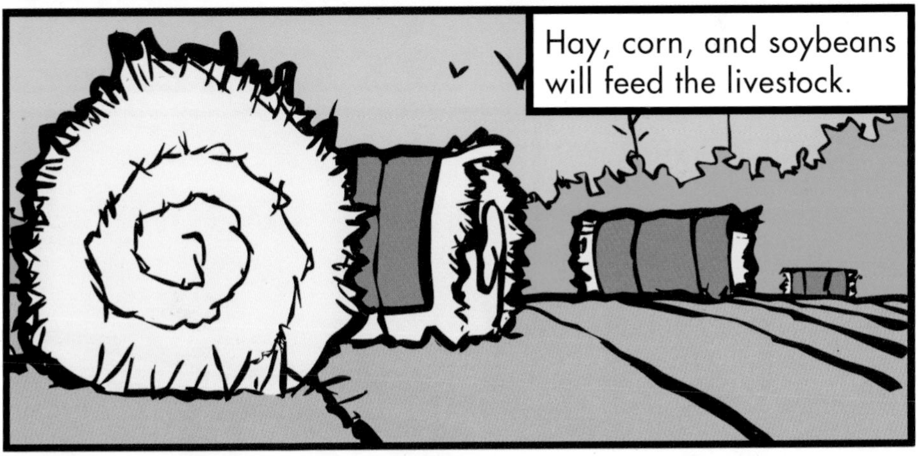
Hay, corn, and soybeans will feed the livestock.

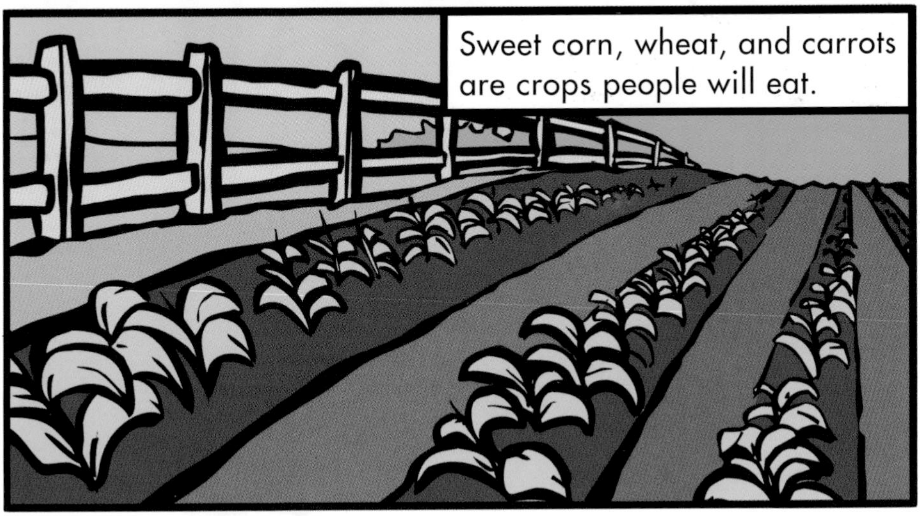
Sweet corn, wheat, and carrots are crops people will eat.

As the crops grow, the farmers weed and irrigate the rows.

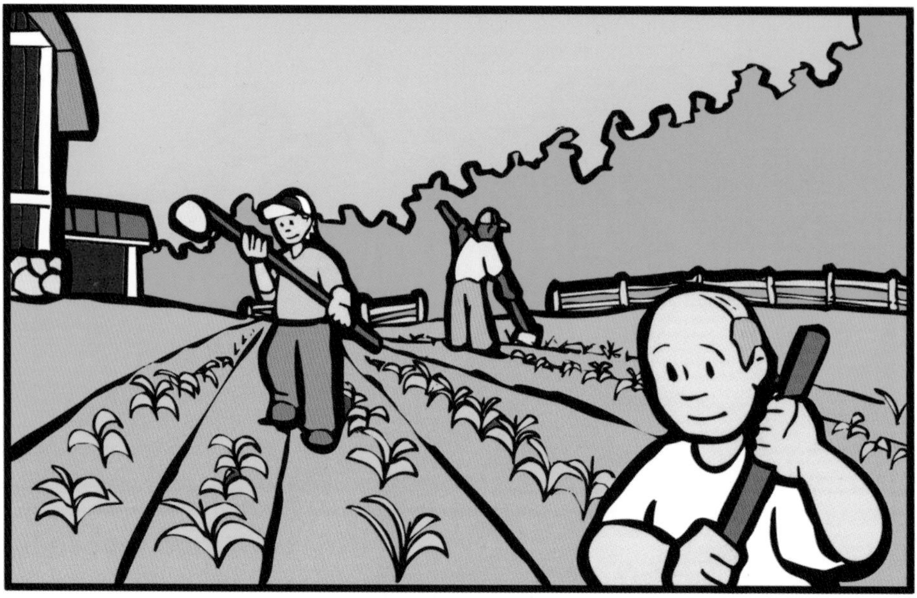

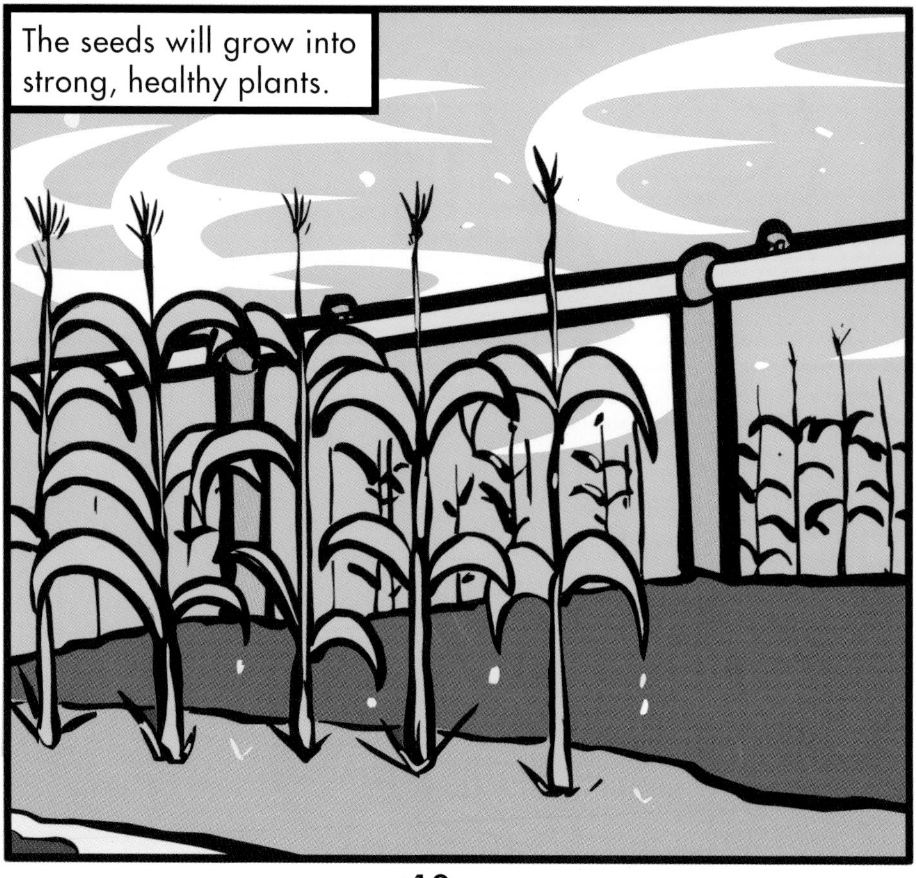
The seeds will grow into strong, healthy plants.

Birds, insects, deer, and other animals try to eat crops. Farmers work to keep the animals out of their fields.

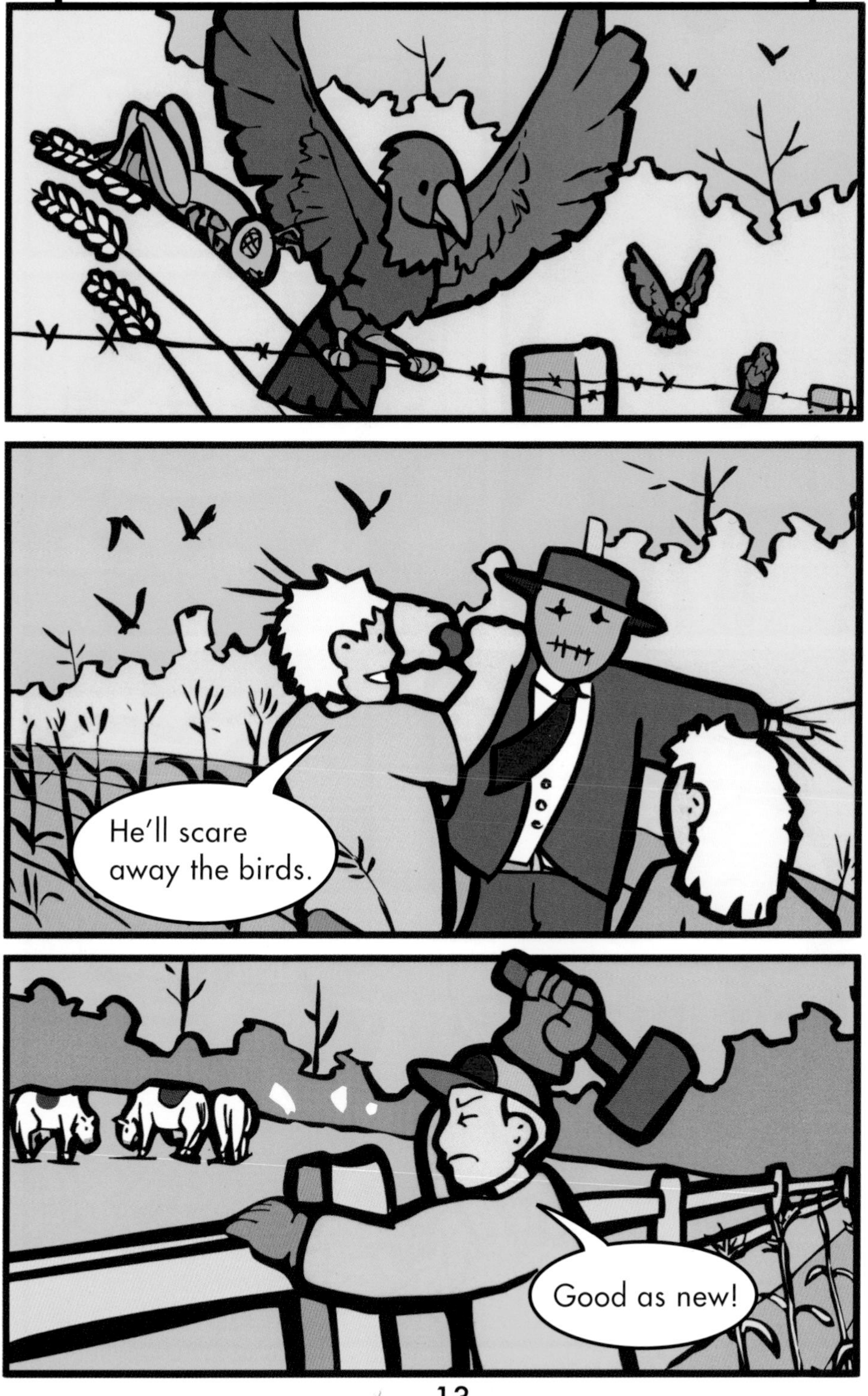
He'll scare away the birds.
Good as new!

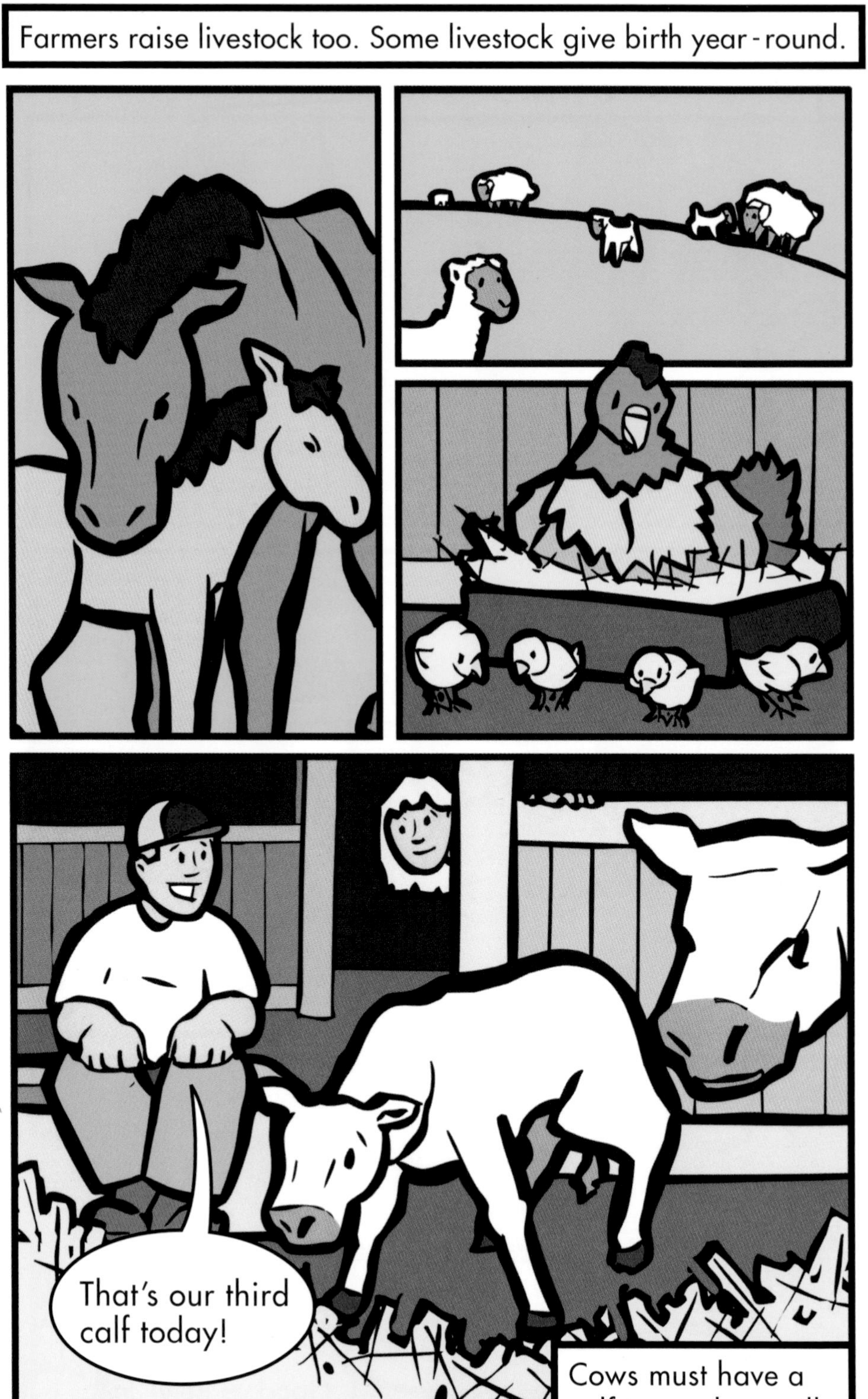
Farmers raise livestock too. Some livestock give birth year-round.
That's our third calf today!
Cows must have a calf to produce milk.

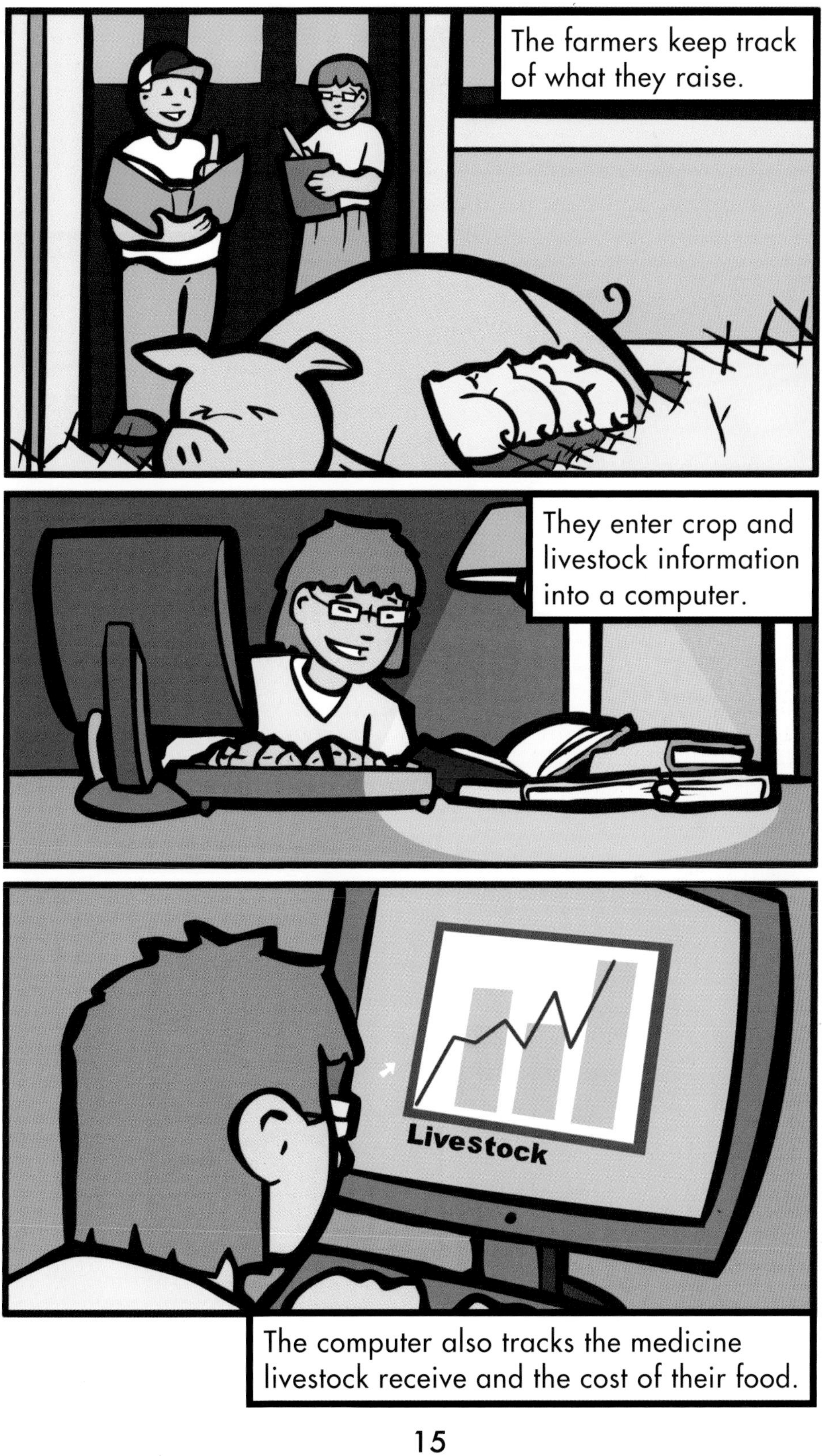
The farmers keep track of what they raise.
They enter crop and livestock information into a computer.
Livestock
The computer also tracks the medicine livestock receive and the cost of their food.

TIME TO HARVEST

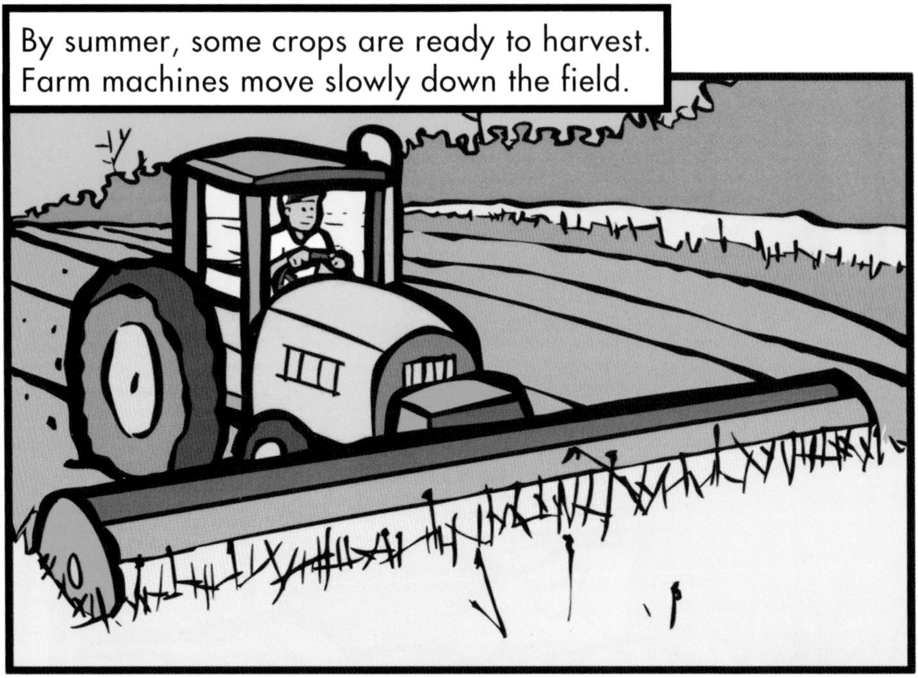
By summer, some crops are ready to harvest. Farm machines move slowly down the field.

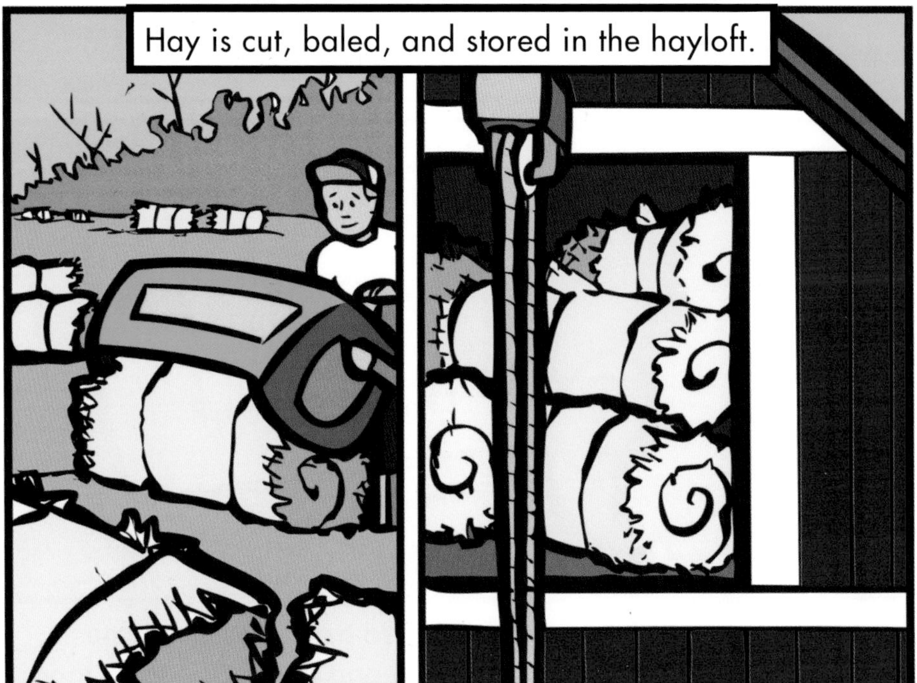
Hay is cut, baled, and stored in the hayloft.

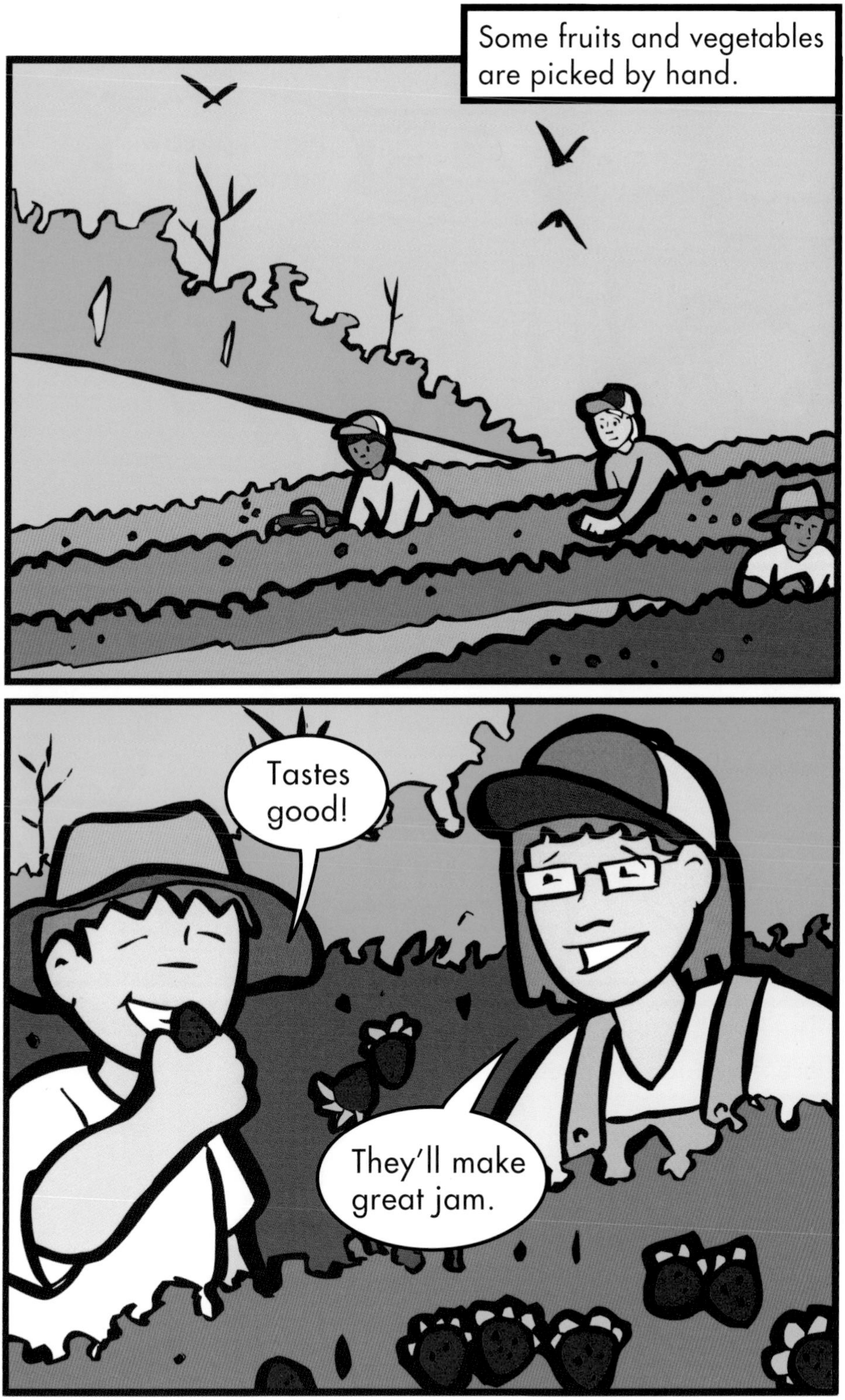
Some fruits and vegetables are picked by hand.
Tastes good!
They'll make great jam.

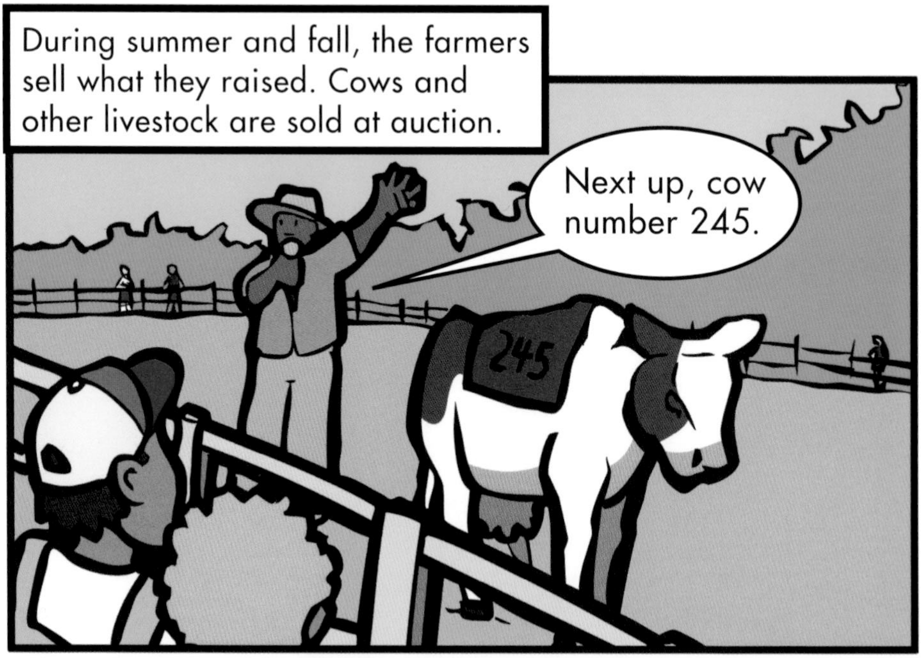
During summer and fall, the farmers sell what they raised. Cows and other livestock are sold at auction.
Next up, cow number 245.
245

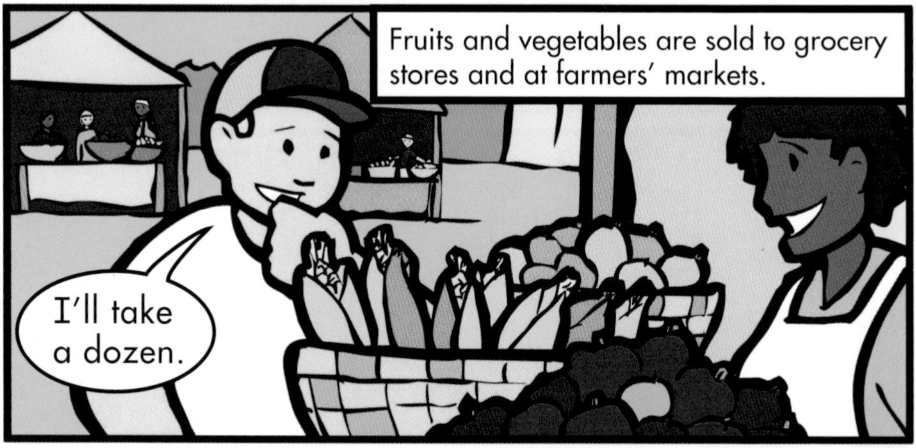
Fruits and vegetables are sold to grocery stores and at farmers' markets.
I'll take a dozen.

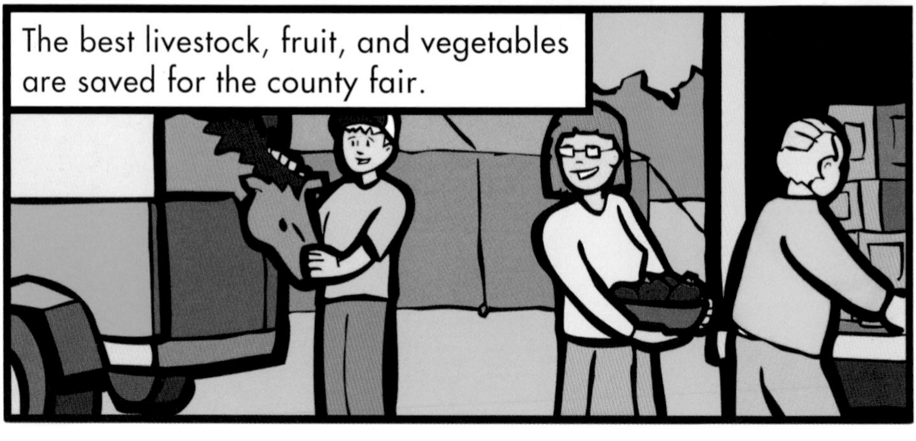
The best livestock, fruit, and vegetables are saved for the county fair.

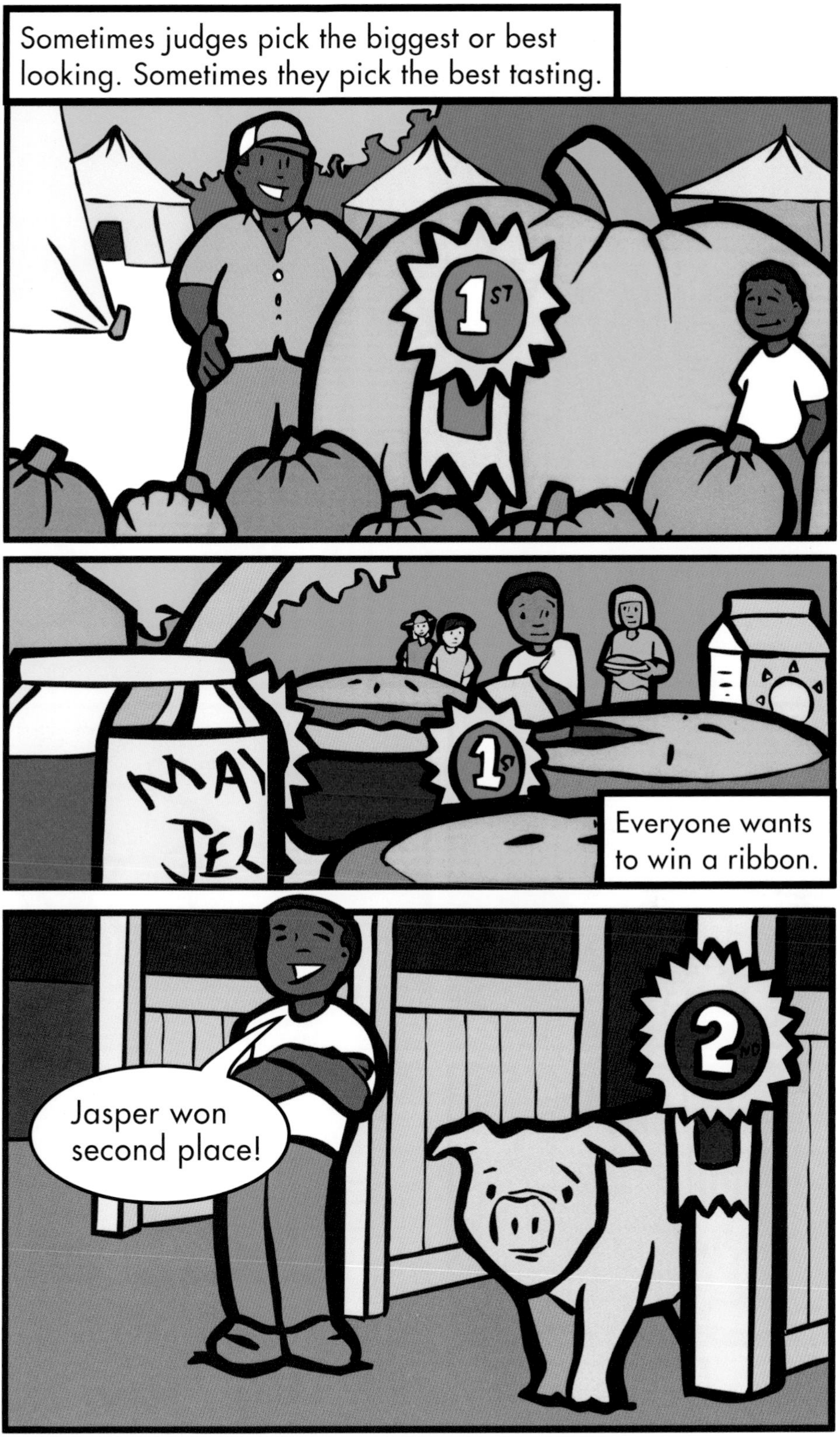
Sometimes judges pick the biggest or best looking. Sometimes they pick the best tasting.
Everyone wants to win a ribbon.
Jasper won second place!

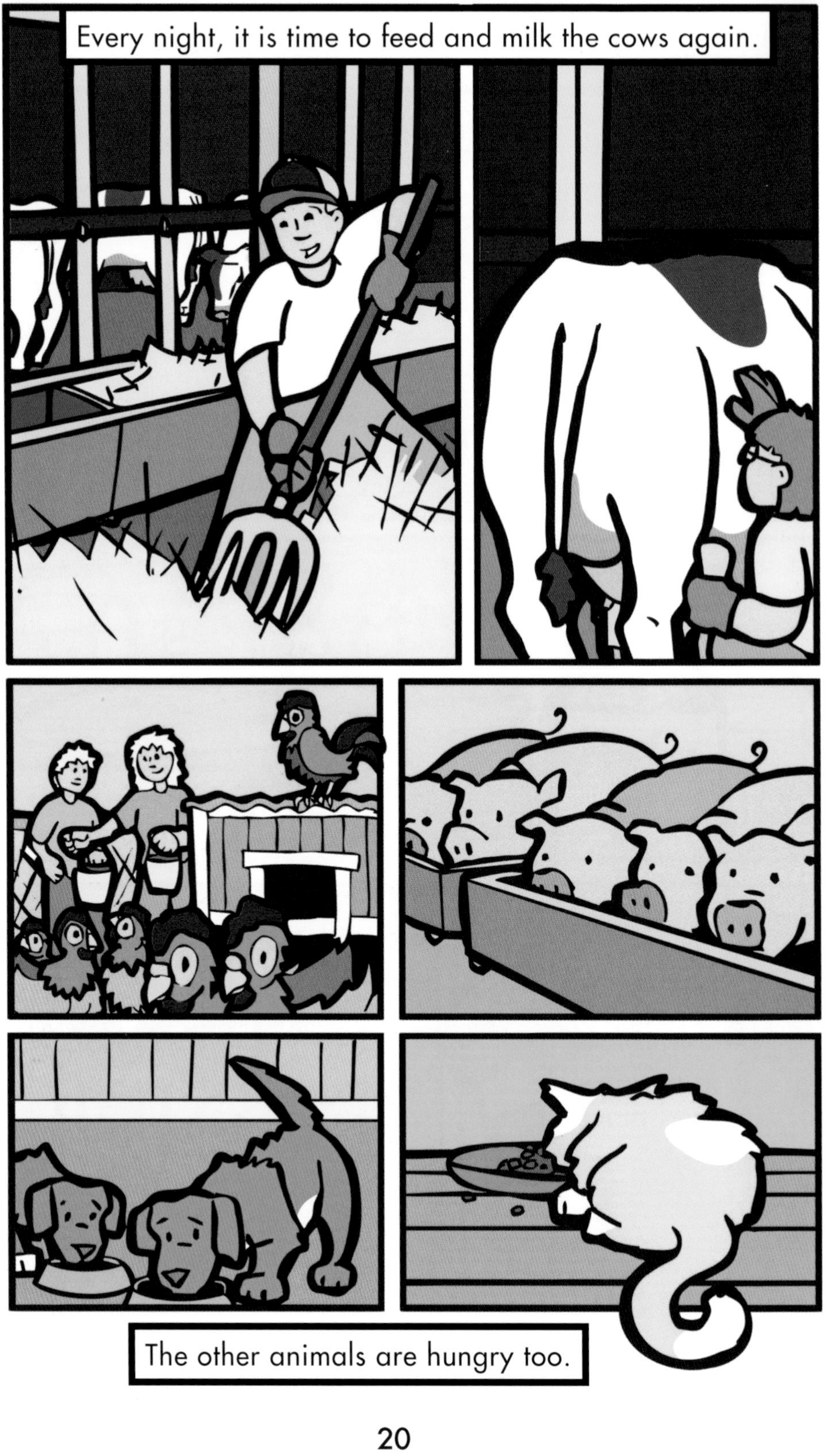
Every night, it is time to feed and milk the cows again.
The other animals are hungry too.

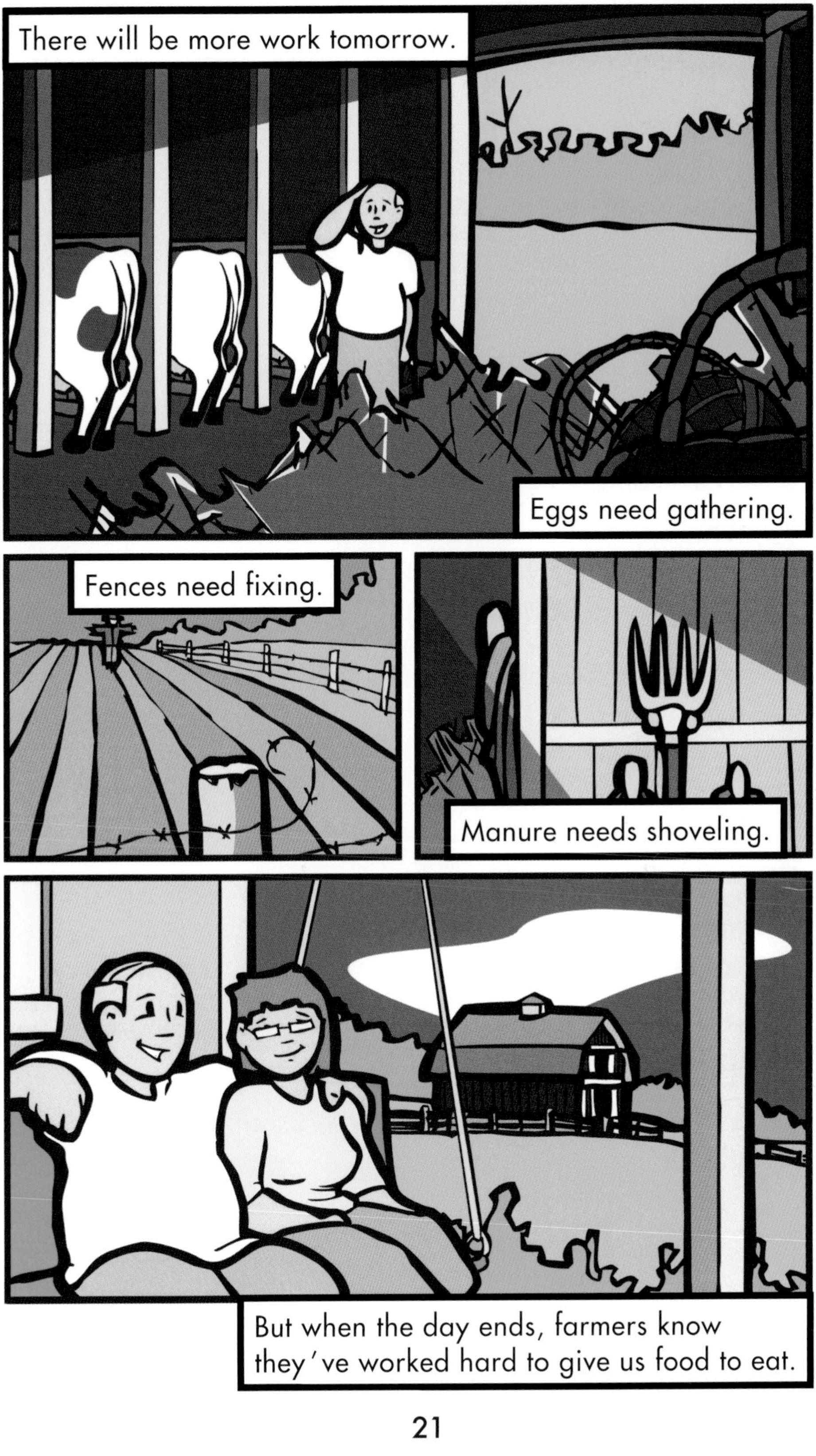
There will be more work tomorrow.
Eggs need gathering.
Fences need fixing.
Manure needs shoveling.
But when the day ends, farmers know they've worked hard to give us food to eat.

GLOSSARY

auction—a public sale where property such as livestock is sold to the highest bidder

chore—a job that has to be done regularly

crop—a plant farmers grow in large amounts, usually for food

fertile—good for growing crops

hayloft—the place where hay is stored in a barn

irrigate—to water dry land

livestock—animals raised on a farm for food and profit

manure—animal waste; some farmers put manure on their fields to make the soil richer

stanchion—a metal gate with two or more bars used to hold cows in place

trough—a long, narrow box used to hold animal feed or water

READ MORE

Dickmann, Nancy. *Jobs on a Farm.* World of Farming. Chicago: Heinemann Library, 2011.

Marsico, Katie. *Working on a Farm.* Ann Arbor, Mich.: Cherry Lake Pub., 2009.

Randall, Jory. *My Day at the Farm.* A Kid's Life. New York: PowerKids Press, 2010.

INTERNET SITES

FactHound offers a safe, fun way to find Internet sites related to this book. All of the sites on FactHound have been researched by our staff.

Here's all you do:

Visit *www.facthound.com*

FactHound will fetch the best sites for you!

INDEX

MY COMMUNITY

TITLES IN THIS SET:

A DAY AT THE **FIRE STATION**

GOING TO THE **DENTIST**

A VISIT TO THE **VET**

WORKING ON THE **FARM**